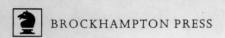
BROCKHAMPTON PRESS

Picture Reference book of the

# ANCIENT GREEKS

General Editor: Boswell Taylor
Illustrator: John Pittaway
Further research by Antony Kamm, MA

## CONTENTS

THE GREAT AGE of the ancient Greeks began about 800 BC, and is generally regarded as having lasted for about 450 years until the death of Alexander the Great in 323 BC, when what had become the Greek Empire was split up. During those 450 years the Greeks helped to shape the future of the world in literature, art, architecture, philosophy and mathematics. They were the first people to develop the idea of democracy, that is government by the people and the freedom of the individual. Until a hundred years ago nothing was known about the Greeks who lived before 800 BC. Homer described the earlier Greeks in his *Iliad* (about the Trojan War) and the *Odyssey* (the wanderings of Odysseus), but these narrative poems were regarded as myths. However, the remarkable discoveries of Heinrich Schliemann at Troy and Mycenae, and of Sir Arthur Evans in Crete, proved many of Homer's descriptions to be accurate. They brought to light two civilizations, the Minoan and the Mycenaean. Even so, there is still today a gap in our knowledge of what happened between the destruction of these civilizations in about 1100 BC and the emergence in about 800 BC of the people whom we call the Greeks.

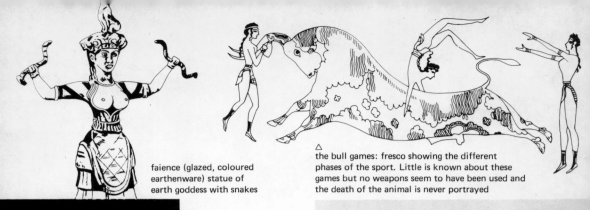

faience (glazed, coloured
earthenware) statue of
earth goddess with snakes

the bull games: fresco showing the different
phases of the sport. Little is known about these
games but no weapons seem to have been used and
the death of the animal is never portrayed

# Crete: the Minoans

the Disc of Phaistos, made of
fired clay and with hieroglyphs
on both sides

◁ Linear B script on a clay tablet.
Linear A and Linear B are the
names given to two different
forms of writing found in Crete

bull's horns on the palace of Minos at
Knossos, marking the place as sacred

presenting offerings;
fresco from sarcophagus
(stone coffin)  ▷

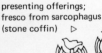

Homer says, 'Out in the dark blue sea there lies a land called
Crete, washed by the waves on every side, densely peopled...
One of the ninety towns is a great city called Knossos, and
there ... King Minos ruled.' Legends tell us that Minos

controlled a vast fleet, kept a fierce bull-like creature to
whom young people were sacrificed, and had in his court a
master-craftsman called Daedalus, who built the labyrinth.
In 1899, under the harsh Mediterranean sun, Evans started

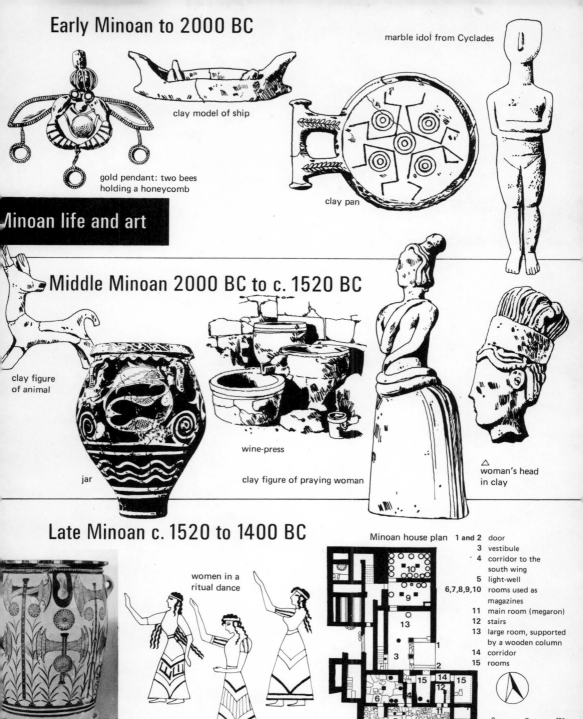

# Early Minoan to 2000 BC

clay model of ship

gold pendant: two bees
holding a honeycomb

marble idol from Cyclades

clay pan

# Middle Minoan 2000 BC to c. 1520 BC

clay figure
of animal

jar

wine-press

clay figure of praying woman

△ woman's head
in clay

# Late Minoan c. 1520 to 1400 BC

women in a
ritual dance

◁ storage jar, decorated
with double axes

Minoan house plan

| | |
|---|---|
| 1 and 2 | door |
| 3 | vestibule |
| 4 | corridor to the south wing |
| 5 | light-well |
| 6,7,8,9,10 | rooms used as magazines |
| 11 | main room (megaron) |
| 12 | stairs |
| 13 | large room, supported by a wooden column |
| 14 | corridor |
| 15 | rooms |

gradually to unearth a complete civilization, unknown before to the modern world. This Minoan culture had lasted, almost unbroken, for 1400 years, from about 2800 BC. The Minoans must have been a seafaring race to withstand invasion for all that time. From wall paintings and other finds, clearly the bull had some religious significance. Some pictures illustrate a ceremony or sport in which young people leapt along a bull's back. The palace at Knossos was

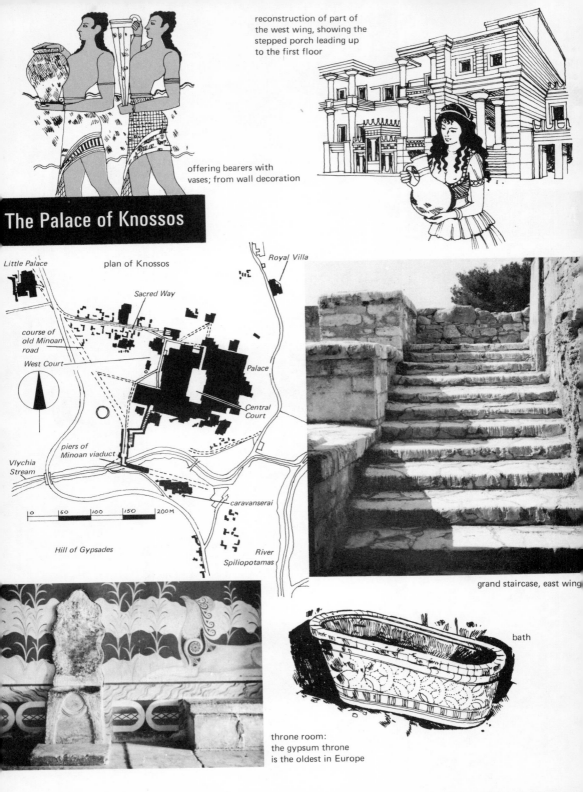

reconstruction of part of
the west wing, showing the
stepped porch leading up
to the first floor

offering bearers with
vases; from wall decoration

# The Palace of Knossos

plan of Knossos

Little Palace

Royal Villa

Sacred Way

course of
old Minoan
road

West Court

Palace

Central
Court

piers of
Minoan viaduct

Vlychia
Stream

0   50   100   150   200M

caravanserai

Hill of Gypsades

River
Spiliopotamas

grand staircase, east wing

bath

throne room:
the gypsum throne
is the oldest in Europe

magnificent, with several storeys, staircases and an elaborate
drainage and sanitary system. The building must have been
designed and built by very skilled craftsmen. Minoan highly
coloured art is altogether different from art of that period
found anywhere else. The Minoans used a decimal numerical
system. About 1400 BC fire ravaged the island of Crete, and
destroyed towns and palaces. This led to a decline of the
Minoan culture.

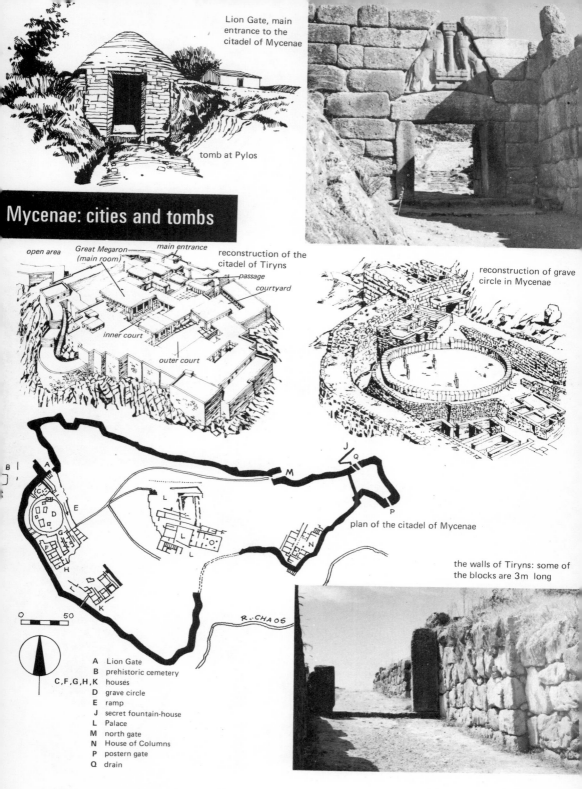

Lion Gate, main entrance to the citadel of Mycenae

tomb at Pylos

# Mycenae: cities and tombs

reconstruction of the citadel of Tiryns

open area

Great Megaron (main room)

main entrance

passage

courtyard

inner court

outer court

reconstruction of grave circle in Mycenae

plan of the citadel of Mycenae

the walls of Tiryns: some of the blocks are 3m long

R. CHAOS

0    50

A   Lion Gate
B   prehistoric cemetery
C,F,G,H,K  houses
D   grave circle
E   ramp
J   secret fountain-house
L   Palace
M   north gate
N   House of Columns
P   postern gate
Q   drain

In 1876 Schliemann, having uncovered many of the secrets of Troy, turned his attentions to Mycenae. This city on the mainland of Greece was said to be 'rich in gold', the legendary home of Agamemnon. Sure enough, he found the gold, and the walls, and much else. He even thought he had found the body of Agamemnon himself, but later discoveries showed that the graves he had dug into were of an even earlier date. These graves, which are known as shaft graves,

◁ woman's head, from a fresco

gold funeral mask of ▷
Mycenaean prince

# Mycenaean life and art

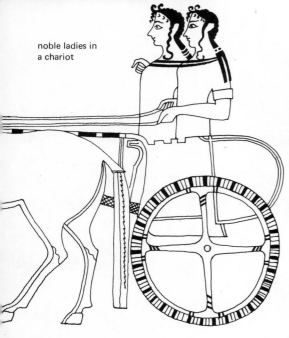
noble ladies in
a chariot

bull caught by its hind
foot; from a gold cup

gold diadem

lead figure of a youth

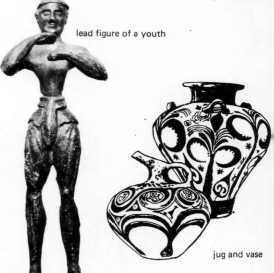
jug and vase

contained jewels, gold and silver. The Mycenaeans, who probably came from the north in about 2000 BC, ruled an empire extending over a large part of the Aegean Sea from about 1400 to 1100 BC. Many of their buildings and their works of art are like those of the Minoans, but as they did not have the protection of the sea, they needed to defend themselves behind massive walls. The Mycenaeans used bronze weapons. A foot-soldier bore a shield, and fought

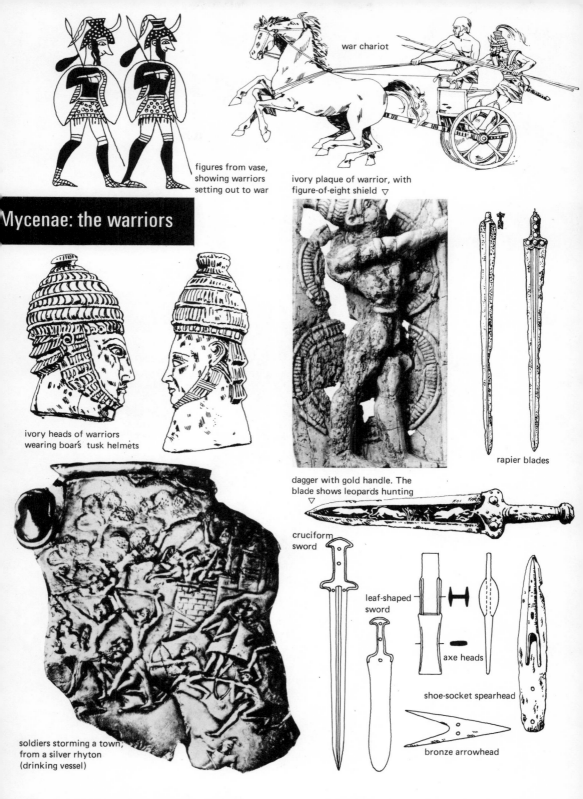

figures from vase,
showing warriors
setting out to war

war chariot

ivory plaque of warrior, with
figure-of-eight shield ▽

ivory heads of warriors
wearing boar's tusk helmets

rapier blades

dagger with gold handle. The
blade shows leopards hunting
▽

cruciform
sword

leaf-shaped
sword

axe heads

shoe-socket spearhead

bronze arrowhead

soldiers storming a town;
from a silver rhyton
(drinking vessel)

with a great thrusting spear or two javelins, which he would hurl at the enemy before rushing in to finish off the job with his sword. The Mycenaeans also used the chariot, which was difficult to manage in the mountainous country of Greece, but which helped to beat the Trojans. Light and easily manoeuvrable, it was drawn by two or four horses. The stone threshold under the Lion Gate still bears the marks of chariot wheels, made at the time of the Trojan War.

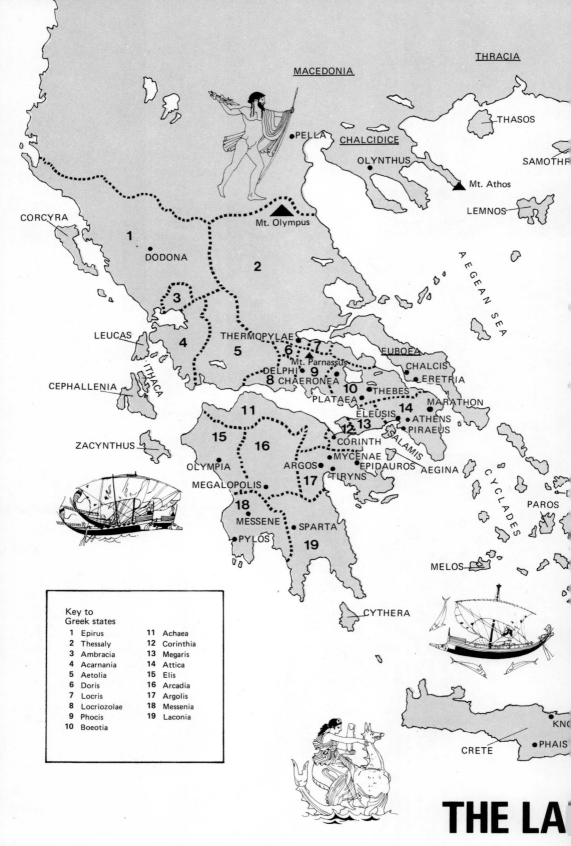

THRACIA

MACEDONIA

THASOS

PELLA

CHALCIDICE

OLYNTHUS

SAMOTHR

Mt. Athos

CORCYRA

1

LEMNOS

DODONA

2

Mt. Olympus

A E G E A N   S E A

3

LEUCAS

4

5

THERMOPYLAE

6   7

EUBOEA

Mt. Parnassus

DELPHI   9

CHALCIS

ERETRIA

CEPHALLENIA

ITHACA

8   CHAERONEA

10   THEBES

PLATAEA

MARATHON

11

ELEUSIS   14   ATHENS

ZACYNTHUS

15

16

12   13

CORINTH

PIRAEUS

SALAMIS

OLYMPIA

ARGOS

MYCENAE

EPIDAUROS

AEGINA

MEGALOPOLIS

17   TIRYNS

C Y C L A D E S

PAROS

18

MESSENE

19

SPARTA

PYLOS

MELOS

CYTHERA

Key to
Greek states

| | | | |
|---|---|---|---|
| 1 | Epirus | 11 | Achaea |
| 2 | Thessaly | 12 | Corinthia |
| 3 | Ambracia | 13 | Megaris |
| 4 | Acarnania | 14 | Attica |
| 5 | Aetolia | 15 | Elis |
| 6 | Doris | 16 | Arcadia |
| 7 | Locris | 17 | Argolis |
| 8 | Locriozolae | 18 | Messenia |
| 9 | Phocis | 19 | Laconia |
| 10 | Boeotia | | |

KNO

CRETE

PHAIS

# THE LA

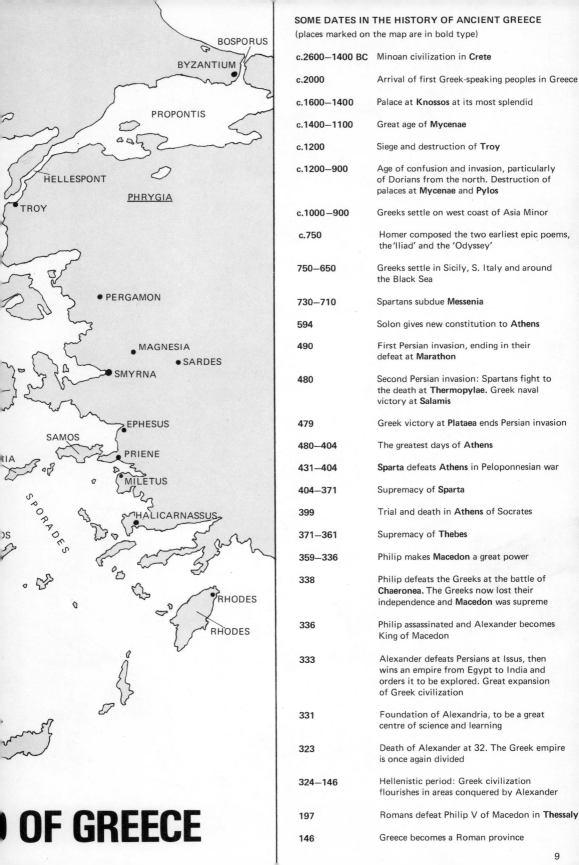

BOSPORUS

BYZANTIUM

PROPONTIS

HELLESPONT

PHRYGIA

TROY

PERGAMON

MAGNESIA

SARDES

SMYRNA

EPHESUS

SAMOS

PRIENE

...RIA

MILETUS

SPORADES

HALICARNASSUS

...OS

RHODES

RHODES

# OF GREECE

## SOME DATES IN THE HISTORY OF ANCIENT GREECE
(places marked on the map are in bold type)

| | |
|---|---|
| c.2600–1400 BC | Minoan civilization in **Crete** |
| c.2000 | Arrival of first Greek-speaking peoples in Greece |
| c.1600–1400 | Palace at **Knossos** at its most splendid |
| c.1400–1100 | Great age of **Mycenae** |
| c.1200 | Siege and destruction of **Troy** |
| c.1200–900 | Age of confusion and invasion, particularly of Dorians from the north. Destruction of palaces at **Mycenae** and **Pylos** |
| c.1000–900 | Greeks settle on west coast of Asia Minor |
| c.750 | Homer composed the two earliest epic poems, the 'Iliad' and the 'Odyssey' |
| 750–650 | Greeks settle in Sicily, S. Italy and around the Black Sea |
| 730–710 | Spartans subdue **Messenia** |
| 594 | Solon gives new constitution to **Athens** |
| 490 | First Persian invasion, ending in their defeat at **Marathon** |
| 480 | Second Persian invasion: Spartans fight to the death at **Thermopylae.** Greek naval victory at **Salamis** |
| 479 | Greek victory at **Plataea** ends Persian invasion |
| 480–404 | The greatest days of **Athens** |
| 431–404 | **Sparta** defeats **Athens** in Peloponnesian war |
| 404–371 | Supremacy of **Sparta** |
| 399 | Trial and death in **Athens** of Socrates |
| 371–361 | Supremacy of **Thebes** |
| 359–336 | Philip makes **Macedon** a great power |
| 338 | Philip defeats the Greeks at the battle of **Chaeronea.** The Greeks now lost their independence and **Macedon** was supreme |
| 336 | Philip assassinated and Alexander becomes King of Macedon |
| 333 | Alexander defeats Persians at Issus, then wins an empire from Egypt to India and orders it to be explored. Great expansion of Greek civilization |
| 331 | Foundation of Alexandria, to be a great centre of science and learning |
| 323 | Death of Alexander at 32. The Greek empire is once again divided |
| 324–146 | Hellenistic period: Greek civilization flourishes in areas conquered by Alexander |
| 197 | Romans defeat Philip V of Macedon in **Thessaly** |
| 146 | Greece becomes a Roman province |

# Athens

△
young men on horseback;
from marble frieze
of the Parthenon at
Athens, 447-432 BC

'Law against Tyranny' passed in  ▷
336 BC, which stated:
'Should anyone, in an attempt at
absolute power, rise up against the
people or try to overthrow the
democracy of Athens — whoever
kills him shall be blameless'

plan of ancient Athens

River Eridanus

Market hill

Agora

Library of Hadrian

Tower of Winds

Roman market place

Themistoclean wall

Hill of Nymphs

Hill of Ares

Acropolis

Pnyx

Theatre of Dionysus

Sanctuary of Olympian Zeus

Stadiur

River Ilissus

0  100  200  300  400  500 M

In about 800 BC, Athens was an ordinary town, no richer
than any of the other Greek cities. Later, Athens became the
most powerful of all the Greek city-states and controlled a
large empire. It was the centre of the ancient world for
philosophy, literature, art, drama, sculpture, building,
engineering, mathematics, naval power, trade and, above all,
for law and democratic rule. During the fifth century BC the
leading statesman of Athens was Pericles, who laid down

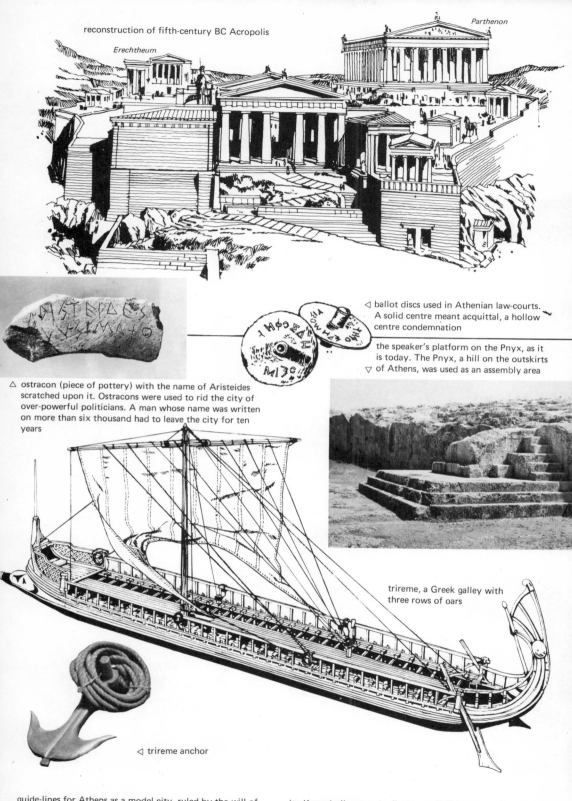

reconstruction of fifth-century BC Acropolis

Erechtheum

Parthenon

◁ ballot discs used in Athenian law-courts. A solid centre meant acquittal, a hollow centre condemnation

the speaker's platform on the Pnyx, as it is today. The Pnyx, a hill on the outskirts ▽ of Athens, was used as an assembly area

△ ostracon (piece of pottery) with the name of Aristeides scratched upon it. Ostracons were used to rid the city of over-powerful politicians. A man whose name was written on more than six thousand had to leave the city for ten years

trireme, a Greek galley with three rows of oars

◁ trireme anchor

guide-lines for Athens as a model city, ruled by the will of the people, who had a share in making and approving laws, in justice and national decisions. Athenians even had the right to vote for the expulsion of unpopular politicians. The city itself was built around a flat-topped hill known as the Acropolis. Beautiful temples and a theatre were built on this hill. These buildings, although partly in ruins, can be seen today.

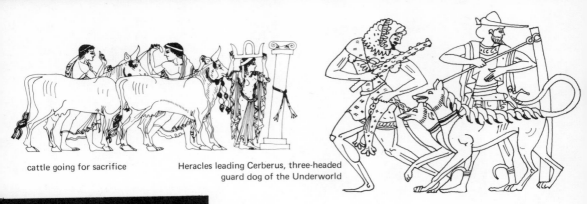

cattle going for sacrifice

Heracles leading Cerberus, three-headed guard dog of the Underworld

# Religion and mythology

Athena the warrior goddess

Homer; probably lived eighth century BC
*reproduced by courtesy of the Museum of Fine Arts, Boston, USA; H.L. Pierce Fund*

Odysseus tempted by the Sirens (nymphs who lured sailors to destruction by their singing) ▽

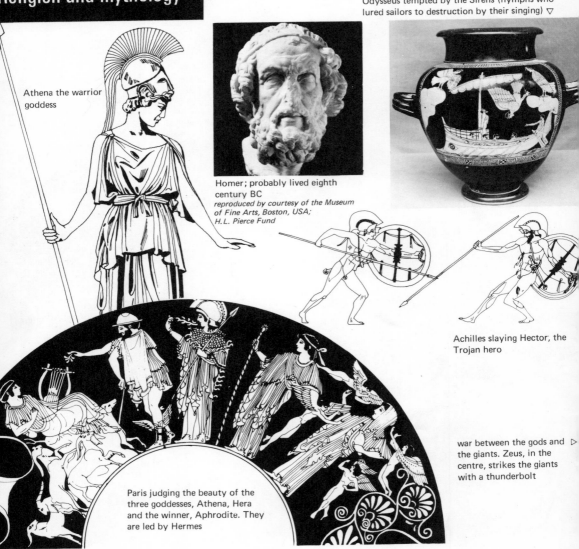

Achilles slaying Hector, the Trojan hero

war between the gods and ▷ the giants. Zeus, in the centre, strikes the giants with a thunderbolt

Paris judging the beauty of the three goddesses, Athena, Hera and the winner, Aphrodite. They are led by Hermes

The religious beliefs of the Greeks were interwoven with the tales of their legendary heroes, many of whom had been immortalized by Homer. From these stories came the idea of the gods having human virtues and failings, and the ability to appear in human or animal form. Many gods, goddesses, spirits and even springs of water, rocks and caves were worshipped and had temples built to them. Cities and trades had their own deities. However, most Greeks agreed that

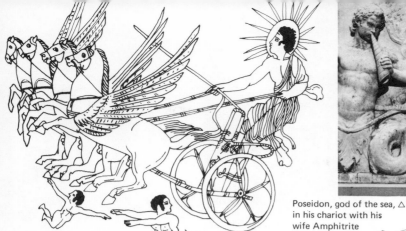

Helios, god of the sun, rising
at dawn, as the stars (represented
by boys) plunge into the sea

Poseidon, god of the sea, △
in his chariot with his
wife Amphitrite

Zeus, in the form of a bull, ▷
carrying off Europa

△
King Aegeus consulting the
oracle at Delphi

Apollo with his lyre ▷

model of
early temple

Atlas and Prometheus
punished by Zeus

Theseus killing the Minotaur (monster
kept in Cretan labyrinth)
▽

Zeus was the supreme ruler of the gods, and that their home
was Mount Olympus. The Greeks were very superstitious.
They believed too in signs and sacrifices, in omens and
oracles. The most famous oracle was at Delphi, and it was
said to give its forecasts in verse. Philosophers used to
question such worship and beliefs. Ordinary people were
satisfied with their traditions, embroidered by any stories
that proved the virtue of their gods.

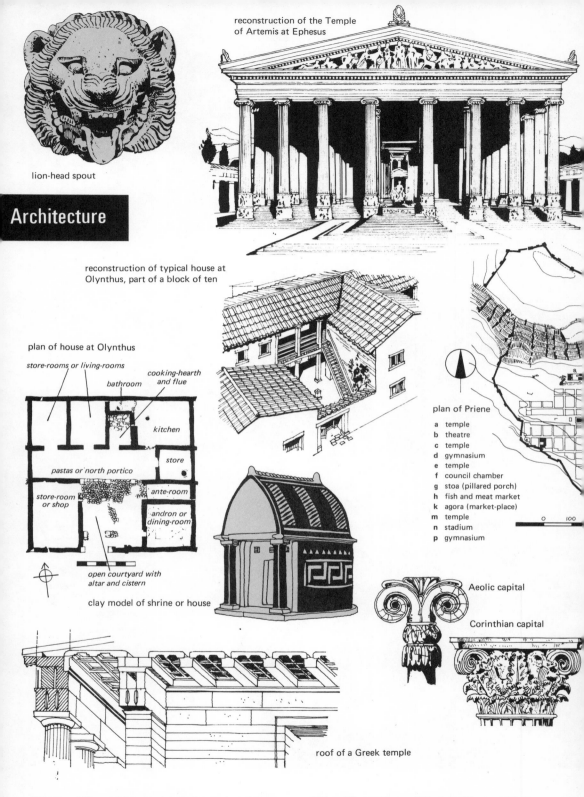

lion-head spout

reconstruction of the Temple of Artemis at Ephesus

# Architecture

reconstruction of typical house at Olynthus, part of a block of ten

plan of house at Olynthus

store-rooms or living-rooms
bathroom
cooking-hearth and flue
kitchen
store
pastas or north portico
store-room or shop
ante-room
andron or dining-room
open courtyard with altar and cistern

clay model of shrine or house

plan of Priene

a temple
b theatre
c temple
d gymnasium
e temple
f council chamber
g stoa (pillared porch)
h fish and meat market
k agora (market-place)
m temple
n stadium
p gymnasium

0          100

Aeolic capital

Corinthian capital

roof of a Greek temple

Minoan and Mycenaean towns were built round a palace or fortress. They were not planned, but just grew. The Greeks of the fifth century designed their towns with streets running either parallel or at right angles. They built large halls in which public meetings could be held. The council hall at Megalopolis was built to seat six thousand. Mycenaean buildings had flat roofs. The Dorians introduced the sloping or gabled roof for temples and the plain, square capital on

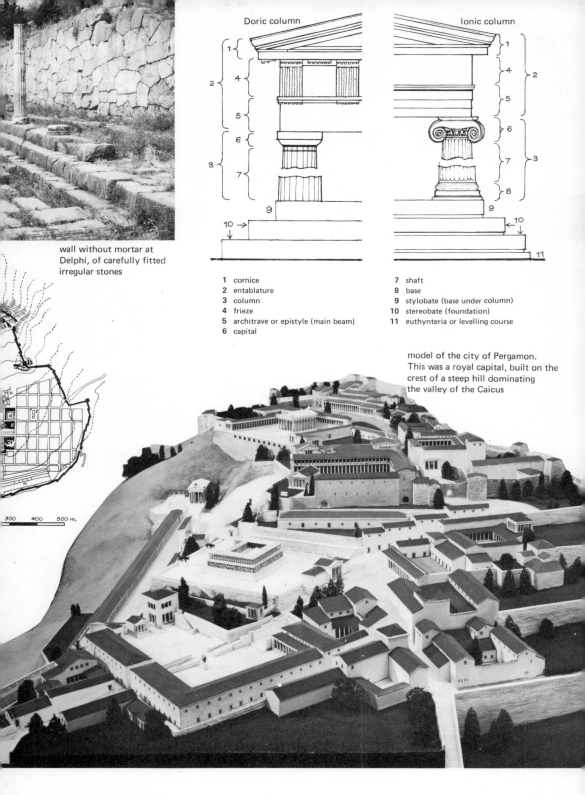

Doric column        Ionic column

wall without mortar at
Delphi, of carefully fitted
irregular stones

1   cornice
2   entablature
3   column
4   frieze
5   architrave or epistyle (main beam)
6   capital

7    shaft
8    base
9    stylobate (base under column)
10   stereobate (foundation)
11   euthynteria or levelling course

300    400    500 m.

model of the city of Pergamon.
This was a royal capital, built on the
crest of a steep hill dominating
the valley of the Caicus

a round base that tops the columns. The Ionians from Asia
Minor brought their style of capital with its curved ends.
The third, heavily decorated style used was known as
Corinthian. The columns not only supported the roof. They

were works of art in themselves. Each one was made to
curve slightly outwards at its middle in order to correct the
optical illusion which would otherwise make it look thinner
at that point.

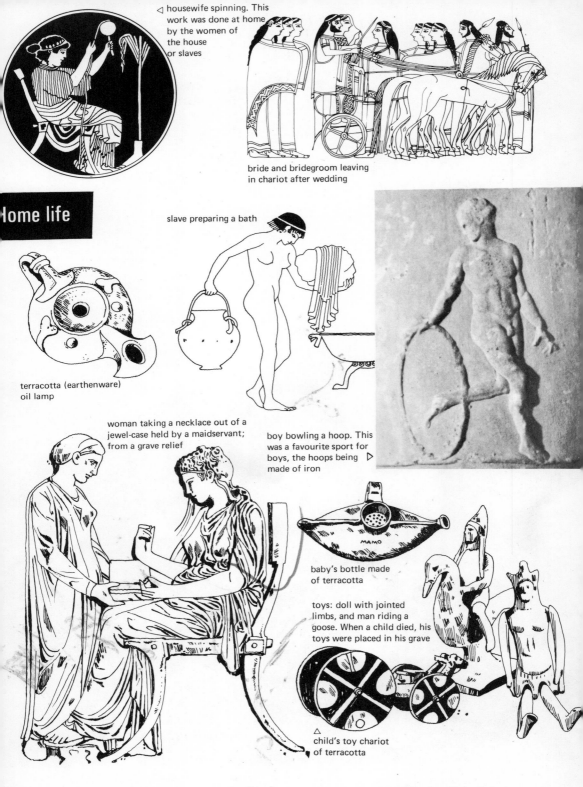

housewife spinning. This work was done at home by the women of the house or slaves

bride and bridegroom leaving in chariot after wedding

## Home life

slave preparing a bath

terracotta (earthenware) oil lamp

woman taking a necklace out of a jewel-case held by a maidservant; from a grave relief

boy bowling a hoop. This was a favourite sport for boys, the hoops being made of iron

baby's bottle made of terracotta

toys: doll with jointed limbs, and man riding a goose. When a child died, his toys were placed in his grave

child's toy chariot of terracotta

In spite of the magnificence of their public buildings, the Greeks lived very simply. Houses of the middle class were made of mud brick walls on a stone base, with timber posts and beams and tiled roofs, and were built round a courtyard with no windows on the outside. There was little furniture. Tables were portable. Chests contained clothes and valuables. There were chairs, beds and stools and men reclined on couches for meals. A wife only ate with her husband when

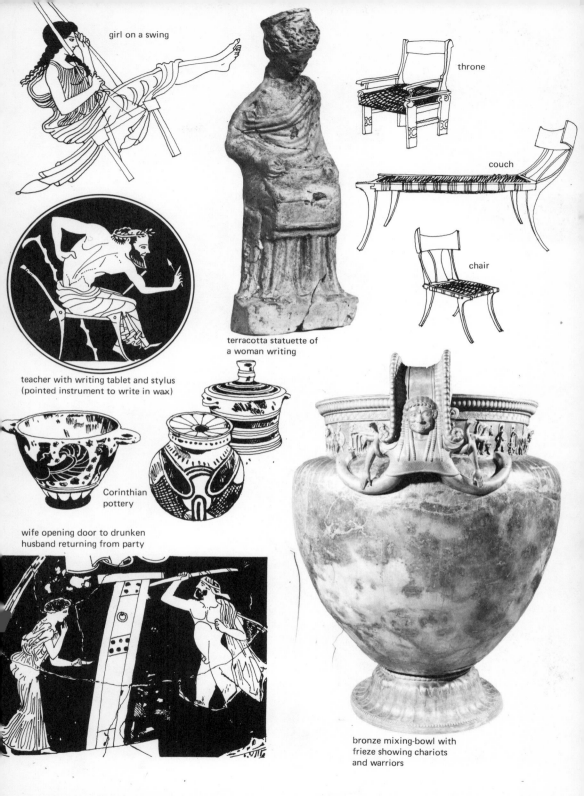

girl on a swing

throne

couch

chair

terracotta statuette of
a woman writing

teacher with writing tablet and stylus
(pointed instrument to write in wax)

Corinthian
pottery

wife opening door to drunken
husband returning from party

bronze mixing-bowl with
frieze showing chariots
and warriors

he had no guests. She would then sit on a chair by his side. While the people described by Homer ate large quantities of meat (whole animals being roasted at a time), the later Greeks did so only after a sacrifice. Their main diet was bread, porridge, broth, fish, olives and other vegetables, and honey. Poorer people ate a kind of sausage made of blood and tripe. Sheep's or goat's milk was drunk, though everyone's usual drink was wine.

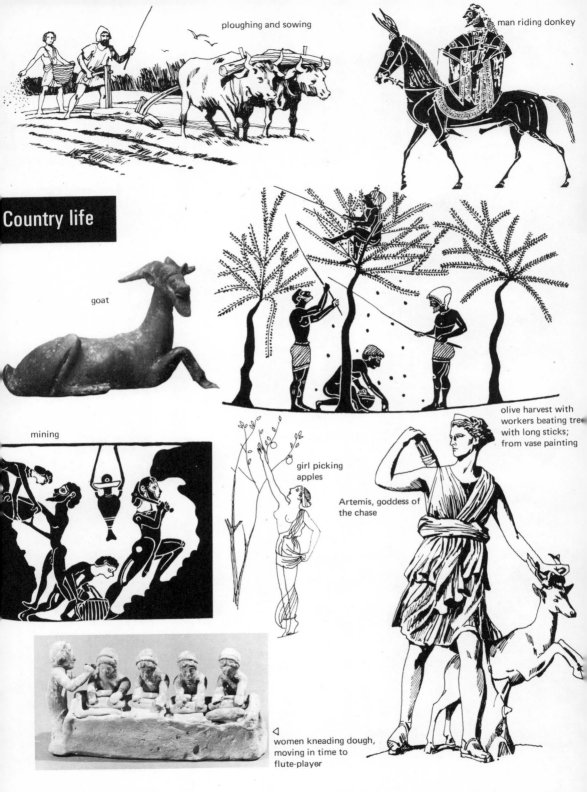

ploughing and sowing

man riding donkey

# Country life

goat

olive harvest with
workers beating tree
with long sticks;
from vase painting

mining

girl picking
apples

Artemis, goddess of
the chase

◁ women kneading dough,
moving in time to
flute-player

Those who lived in the country did not regard themselves as permanent country folk, since at times of war they took refuge within the walls of the nearest town. The main produce was corn, wine and olives, which were eaten as a vegetable and also pressed to make oil. Ploughs were used to break up the hard ground; digging was done with a mattock. Flower gardens must have existed to supply flowers for wreaths and garlands for festivals.

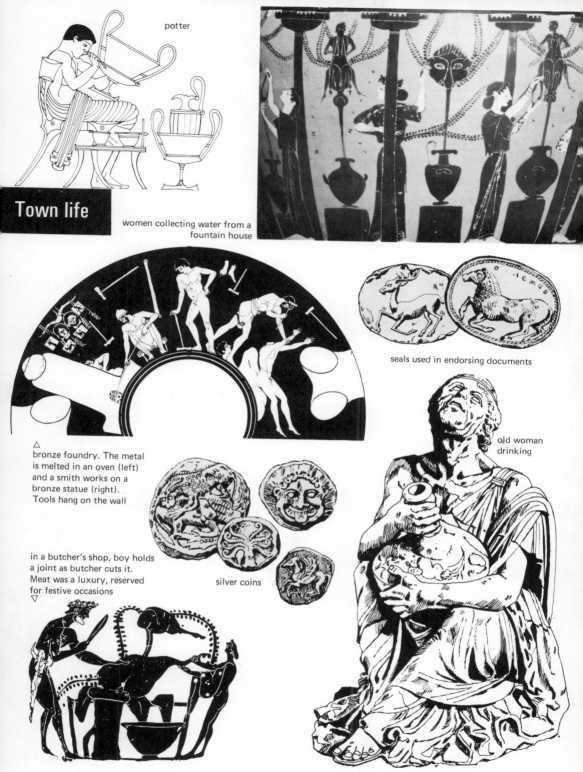

potter

women collecting water from a fountain house

# Town life

bronze foundry. The metal is melted in an oven (left) and a smith works on a bronze statue (right). Tools hang on the wall

seals used in endorsing documents

old woman drinking

in a butcher's shop, boy holds a joint as butcher cuts it. Meat was a luxury, reserved for festive occasions

silver coins

The Greek town, with its narrow streets, was built round its agora, the market or meeting-place where townspeople and countrymen gathered for formal public meetings, for trading or simply for conversation. Wealthy men lived ordered, almost leisurely lives. They would take exercise in the morning or visit friends before going to the agora or walking in the porticoes that surrounded it. After a light midday dinner they would take more exercise or visit the baths.

drawing of an Athenian
warrior c.690 BC

male Phrygian costume
c.230 BC

△ girls putting on the chiton, a single
piece of cloth worn by both men and women

## costume

hairstyles

bronze
mirror case

necklace

young girl

bronze statuette of
a woman wearing a
peplos (skirt) with a
decorated border
▽

boy in
a cloak

terracotta statuette of young
woman wearing tunic, cloak and
sun hat. She is holding a fan

pyxis or
jewel box ▽

earrings

Clothes were simple. Men wore a shirt-like chiton and on top a garment of wool or skins. Women also wore the chiton, over which they draped an outer wrap. In later times a woollen or linen chiton was worn, short or long, by men and women, with a girdle which gathered in the lower part. The outer garment was like a shawl. At first men wore long hair and beards, though short hair later prevailed. The Macedonians introduced shaving during the fourth century.

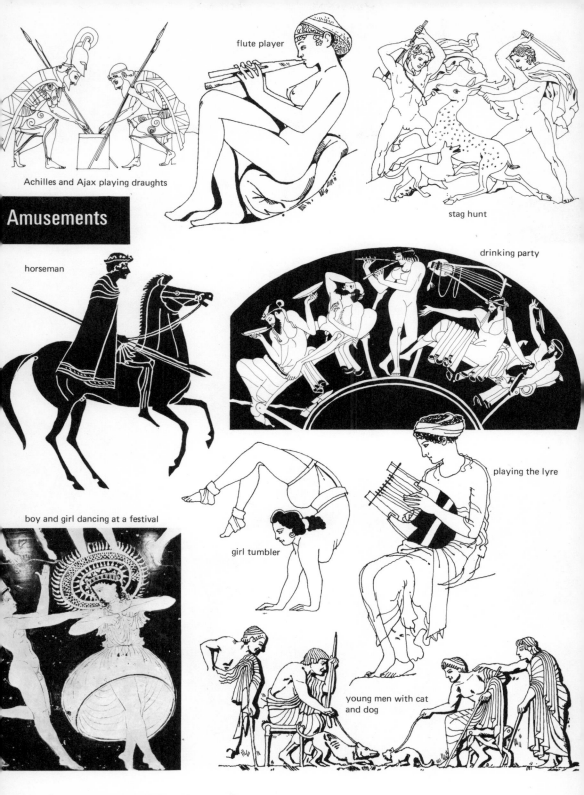

Achilles and Ajax playing draughts

flute player

stag hunt

# Amusements

horseman

drinking party

boy and girl dancing at a festival

girl tumbler

playing the lyre

young men with cat and dog

The chief country amusement was hunting deer, hares and boars, using dogs and nets, and spears or bows. Ball games were played involving throwing and catching. Forms of tennis and hockey are also seen in paintings and sculptures.

There were indoor games of knuckle-bones and dice, while after dinner men amused themselves with word games and with cottabus, a game in which wine dregs were tossed from a bowl at a target.

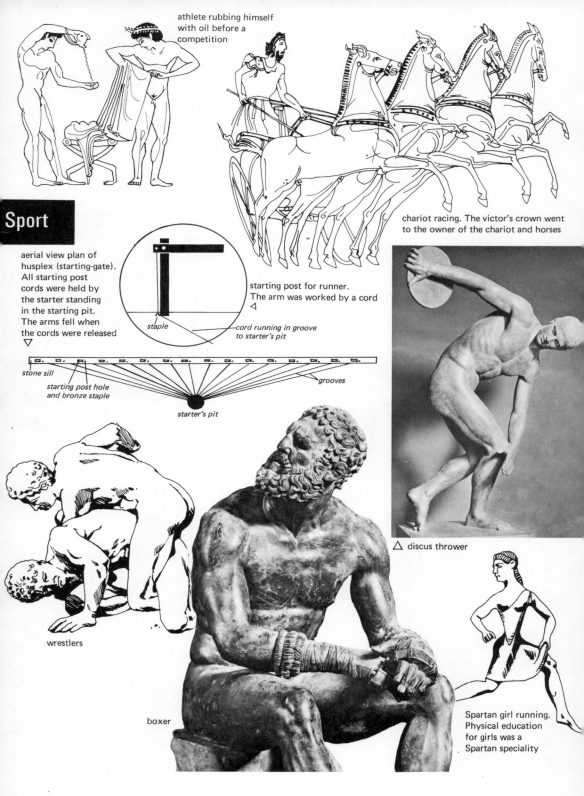

athlete rubbing himself with oil before a competition

chariot racing. The victor's crown went to the owner of the chariot and horses

# Sport

aerial view plan of husplex (starting-gate). All starting post cords were held by the starter standing in the starting pit. The arms fell when the cords were released ▽

staple

starting post for runner. The arm was worked by a cord ◁

cord running in groove to starter's pit

stone sill

starting post hole and bronze staple

grooves

starter's pit

discus thrower

wrestlers

boxer

Spartan girl running. Physical education for girls was a Spartan speciality

Athletics, boxing, gymnastics and wrestling were important in Greek life. There were four national religious festivals in which athletic games played a large part. The most famous of these were the Olympic Games, which were held every

fourth year continuously from 776 BC. A sacred truce was called for a fortnight before and after the games. The main sports at Olympia were discus, javelin, wrestling, long jump (which was probably more like the modern triple jump, with

22

runners

jumper landing

umpire

javelin thrower

plan of a stadium. All runners made a left-hand turn at the post, so those at A would have the most difficult run

A
start and finish
B
C
turning post

athlete clearing stadium of stones

Olympia

1  gymnasium
2  temple of Hera
3  temple of Zeus Olympius
4  race course

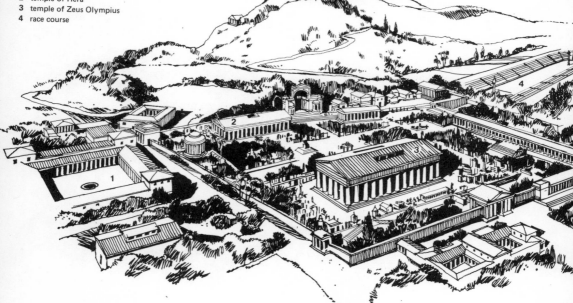

competitors carrying weights in their hands to gain momentum), and running. Runners began the race from behind a kind of starting-gate, getting their initial push from grooves into which they fitted their toes. There was a sprint of 365 metres: up the track, a sharp turn round a post at the end, and back again. There was also a long-distance race. At various times the Olympics included boxing, chariot-racing, running in armour and competitions for boys.

men of the chorus
on horseback

the playwright Menander (342-292 BC),
with some of his masks

the dramatist Sophocles (c.496-406 BC)

reconstruction of the theatre
at Priene, which seated over
5,000 people
▽

△ scene from *The Eumenides* by the tragedian
Aeschylus (525-456 BC); from a vase painting

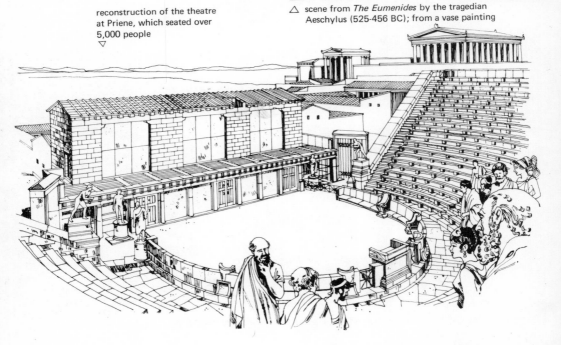

Greek drama also had a religious significance, and developed
from songs and dances performed in honour of a god. Steps
would be built up a hillside to seat spectators, or the dancers
might be carried on a travelling stage. During the fifth

century special open-air theatres began to be built. At about
the same time the dances gave way to plays, the forerunners
of the great tragedies of Aeschylus, Sophocles and Euripides,
and the comedies of Aristophanes. There were up to three

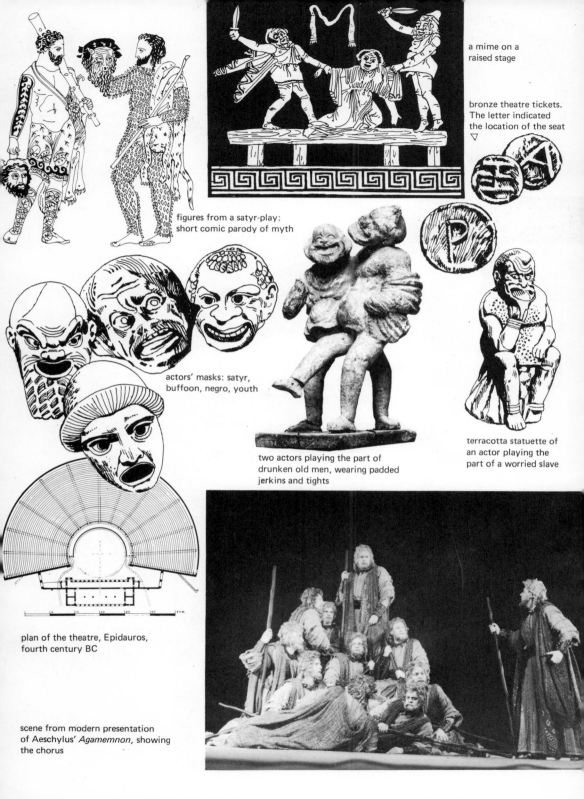

a mime on a raised stage

bronze theatre tickets. The letter indicated the location of the seat ▽

figures from a satyr-play: short comic parody of myth

actors' masks: satyr, buffoon, negro, youth

two actors playing the part of drunken old men, wearing padded jerkins and tights

terracotta statuette of an actor playing the part of a worried slave

plan of the theatre, Epidauros, fourth century BC

scene from modern presentation of Aeschylus' *Agamemnon*, showing the chorus

actors in a play, always men, who wore different masks to portray the many different characters. The chorus recited behind the actors, giving the background to the action. Greeks often used mythology for their plots, with stories, for instance, of Agamemnon, Oedipus, Hercules and Dionysus. In the festivals of plays, the dramatists competed for a prize, awarded by a jury chosen by lot from the ordinary spectators.

25

young rider by the painter Euphronios c.500 BC

horse's head of marble from the Parthenon c.435 BC

bronze figure of a charioteer c.480 BC

the Sleeping Ariadne c.240 BC

marble statue of a Gaul killing his wife and himself to avoid capture; copy of a Greek work of c.230

bronze griffin head from Olympia c.650 BC

marble statue of Leda; Roman copy of Greek original of 370 BC

statue of Aphrodite, the 'Venus de Milo'

sixth-century drawing of Odysseus escaping from Polyphemus

# Art and sculpture

The Greeks appreciated art as much as they appreciated drama, sport and the beauty of movement and of the human body. Indeed two of their most famous sculptors, Pythagoras and Myron, are best known for their statues of athletes in action. This perfection of form was achieved by the middle of the fifth century, and it has influenced sculptors ever since. Sculpture was for the public to gaze at, and apart from many statues of the gods which adorned temples, there were

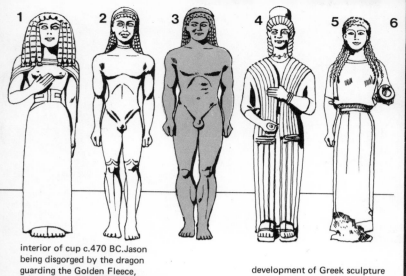

interior of cup c.470 BC. Jason being disgorged by the dragon guarding the Golden Fleece, and Athena

development of Greek sculpture

1. grey limestone female figure c.650 BC
2. marble figure of youth c.600 BC
3. marble statue c.520 BC
4. marble figure of woman holding pomegranate, early 6th cent. BC
5. marble figure of girl in chiton and peplos c.530 BC
6. marble figure of girl in sleeved chiton and cloak, late 6th century BC

part of the frieze from the Altar of Zeus at Pergamon, c.180 BC, showing Athena in combat

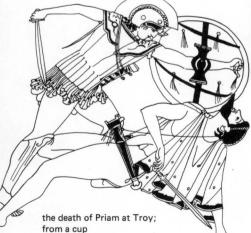

the death of Priam at Troy; from a cup

◁ Medusa, from temple of Artemis in Corfu (early 6th century BC)

many public monuments depicting war and religious festivals. The frieze right round the outside of the temple-chamber of the Parthenon on the Acropolis of Athens was 160 metres long and represents the Panathenaic procession, part of the great national festival in honour of Athena, patroness of the city. Though Greek artists did painting and murals, little of this work has survived. But many of their remarkable vase paintings can still be seen.

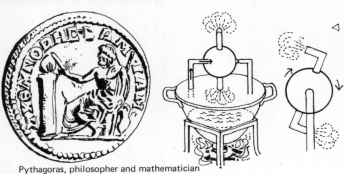

Pythagoras, philosopher and mathematician
of the sixth century BC, on a coin from Samos, his birthplace

◁ a machine, as described
by Hero. Steam passes
through a pipe into a
hollow globe and escapes
through other pipes,
making the globe revolve

the Chalcidian alphabet ▷
of western Greece
scratched on a toy jug

# Knowledge and learning

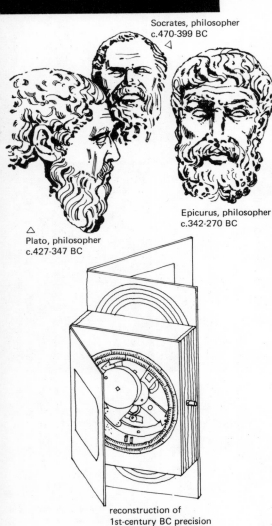

Socrates, philosopher
c.470-399 BC
◁

Epicurus, philosopher
c.342-270 BC

△
Plato, philosopher
c.427-347 BC

reconstruction of
1st-century BC precision
instrument used in astronomy

| GREEK ALPHABET LETTER | | NAME OF LETTER | ENGLISH TRANS-LITERATION | GREEK WORD TAKEN INTO MODERN ENGLISH USAGE |
|---|---|---|---|---|
| A | α | alpha | a | architect |
| B | β | beta | b | blasphemy |
| Γ | γ | gamma | g | gangrene |
| Δ | δ | delta | d | diagnosis |
| E | ε | epsilon | e | epilogue |
| Z | ζ | zeta | z | Zodiac |
| H | η | eta | e | hero** |
| Θ | θ | theta | th | theorem |
| I | ι | iota | i | hippopotamus** |
| K | κ | kappa | k | catastrophe |
| Λ | λ | lambda | l | lion |
| M | μ | mu | m | mathematics |
| N | ν | nu | n | nymph |
| Ξ | ξ | xi | x (ks) | xenophobia |
| O | ο | omicron | o | orchestra |
| Π | π | pi | p | parallel |
| P | ρ | rho | r | rhetoric |
| Σ | σ* s† | sigma | s | sympathy |
| T | τ | tau | t | tactics |
| Y | υ | upsilon | u, y | hypothesis** |
| Φ | φ | phi | ph | physical |
| X | χ | chi | kh,ch | chaos |
| Ψ | ψ | psi | ps | psyche |
| Ω | ω | omega | o | ode |

* at beginning or
in middle of word    † at end of word

** no separate
letter for 'h'

One of the things the Greeks greatly improved upon was the
alphabet, which was of Semitic origin. Greek dramatists and
poets created fine literature. Their historians have equal
importance, for much of our knowledge of those days is
derived from them. Herodotus is our main source of
information about the Persian wars and the battles of
Salamis, Marathon and Thermopylae. From Thucydides we
have among many other events the funeral speech of Pericles

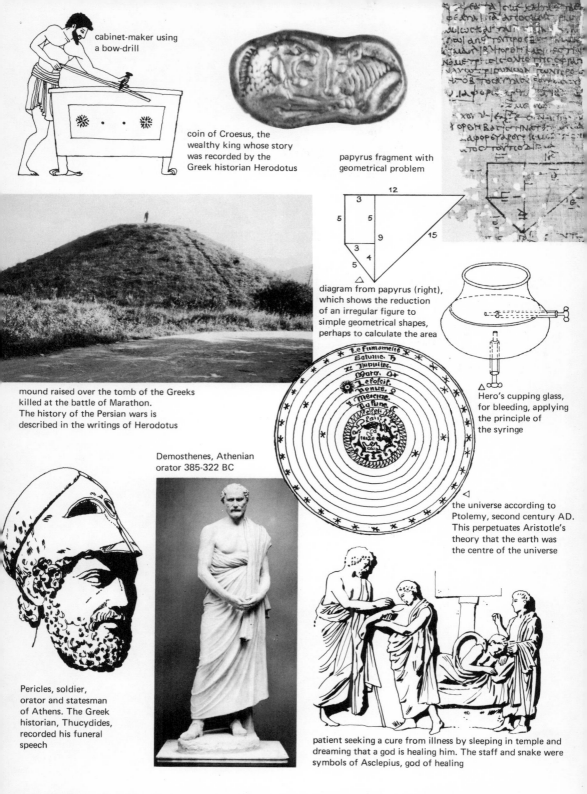

cabinet-maker using a bow-drill

coin of Croesus, the wealthy king whose story was recorded by the Greek historian Herodotus

papyrus fragment with geometrical problem

diagram from papyrus (right), which shows the reduction of an irregular figure to simple geometrical shapes, perhaps to calculate the area

mound raised over the tomb of the Greeks killed at the battle of Marathon. The history of the Persian wars is described in the writings of Herodotus

Hero's cupping glass, for bleeding, applying the principle of the syringe

Demosthenes, Athenian orator 385-322 BC

the universe according to Ptolemy, second century AD. This perpetuates Aristotle's theory that the earth was the centre of the universe

Pericles, soldier, orator and statesman of Athens. The Greek historian, Thucydides, recorded his funeral speech

patient seeking a cure from illness by sleeping in temple and dreaming that a god is healing him. The staff and snake were symbols of Asclepius, god of healing

and the accurate account of a disastrous Athenian expedition to Syracuse. Also through writings we have the words and thoughts of the early philosophers, Plato and Socrates. Pythagoras and Archimedes have given us mathematical theorems. The Greeks gave to the modern world the principles of the gear, the pulley and the screw; of astronomy, medicine and natural sciences. Indeed, after Aristotle little further advance in zoology or botany was made for 1800 years.

# War

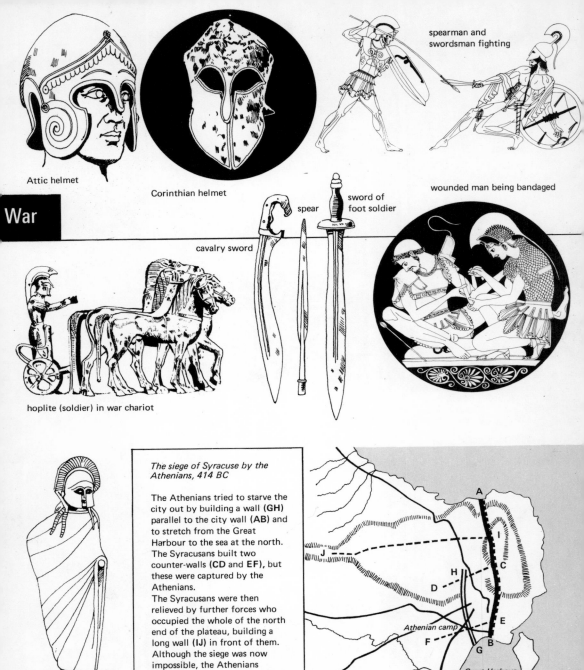

Attic helmet

Corinthian helmet

spearman and swordsman fighting

wounded man being bandaged

cavalry sword

spear

sword of foot soldier

hoplite (soldier) in war chariot

Spartan soldier in cloak and Corinthian helmet

*The siege of Syracuse by the Athenians, 414 BC*

The Athenians tried to starve the city out by building a wall (GH) parallel to the city wall (AB) and to stretch from the Great Harbour to the sea at the north. The Syracusans built two counter-walls (CD and EF), but these were captured by the Athenians.
The Syracusans were then relieved by further forces who occupied the whole of the north end of the plateau, building a long wall (IJ) in front of them. Although the siege was now impossible, the Athenians lingered on, and were defeated in the following year.

Athenian camp

Great Harbour

—— roads

～～ rivers

The Greeks were fine seamen. At first a sea-fight was fought like a land battle, with soldiers fighting from the decks while their ships remained stationary. A true form of naval warfare was developed during the fifth century, when the fast triremes, with their triple banks of oars, came to be regarded more as missiles to charge the enemy and ram them or else manoeuvre them into difficult water. On land the Spartan hoplites (heavily-armed soldiers) proved invincible until it

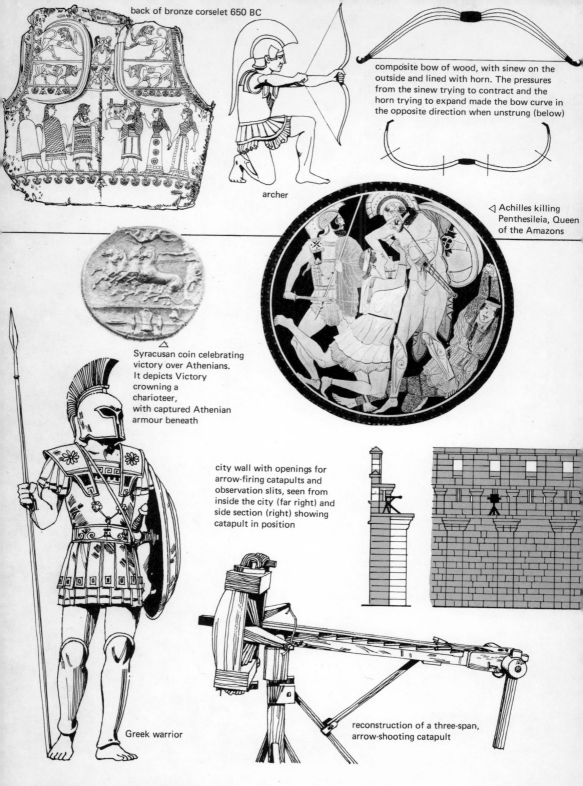

back of bronze corselet 650 BC

archer

composite bow of wood, with sinew on the outside and lined with horn. The pressures from the sinew trying to contract and the horn trying to expand made the bow curve in the opposite direction when unstrung (below)

◁ Achilles killing Penthesileia, Queen of the Amazons

△ Syracusan coin celebrating victory over Athenians. It depicts Victory crowning a charioteer, with captured Athenian armour beneath

city wall with openings for arrow-firing catapults and observation slits, seen from inside the city (far right) and side section (right) showing catapult in position

Greek warrior

reconstruction of a three-span, arrow-shooting catapult

was discovered that light-armed troops were more effective in hilly or muddy country. On occasions the Persians would hire Greek mercenaries to fight against another state or in their own domestic wars. All the best of Greek fighting methods, the hoplite, the phalanx (a closely-ranked body of men bearing immense spears), the siege engines, were finally used together by Alexander the Great, whose conquests ranged over the whole of Greece, Asia Minor and beyond.

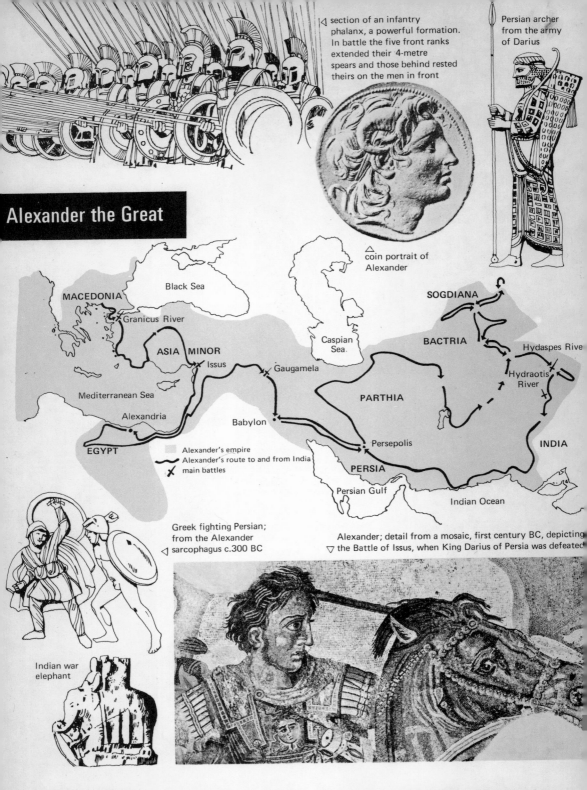

section of an infantry phalanx, a powerful formation. In battle the five front ranks extended their 4-metre spears and those behind rested theirs on the men in front

Persian archer from the army of Darius

# Alexander the Great

coin portrait of Alexander

MACEDONIA

Black Sea

Granicus River

ASIA MINOR

Issus

Gaugamela

Caspian Sea

SOGDIANA

BACTRIA

Hydaspes Rive

Hydraotis River

Mediterranean Sea

PARTHIA

Alexandria

Babylon

Persepolis

INDIA

EGYPT

Alexander's empire
Alexander's route to and from India
main battles

PERSIA

Persian Gulf

Indian Ocean

Greek fighting Persian; from the Alexander sarcophagus c.300 BC

Alexander; detail from a mosaic, first century BC, depicting the Battle of Issus, when King Darius of Persia was defeated

Indian war elephant

Alexander succeeded to his father's kingdom of Macedon in 336 BC at the age of about 20. When he died 13 years later he had changed the face of the world. He defeated the Greek states, then the might of Persia, and marched on east into

India, extending his empire as he went. He founded the city of Alexandria, which was for many years to be the centre of learning. For the first time the Greeks were united as one kingdom. The era of the independent city-states was over.